Where Was the Room Where It Happened?

The Unofficial
Hamilton: An American Musical
Location Guide

B.L. Barreras

D0286030

©2016 B.L. Barreras

Song titles, song excerpts and books mentioned herein are the copyrighted property of their respective owners.

All rights reserved. No part of this book may be reproduced, in any form or by any means without permission in writing from the author.

Printed in the United States of America

First printing

This book is dedicated to my wonderful wife, Rebecca, and to my great kids, London and Andrew, who may actually love Hamilton *more than I do. I couldn't have done this without their support.*

TABLE OF CONTENTS

ABOUT THIS BOOK

This book's primary purpose is to provide additional information about the locations that are used and/or mentioned in *Hamilton: An American Musical*. This is made somewhat difficult by the fact that Lin-Manuel Miranda, in crafting what my family and I think is the greatest Broadway show ever, creates scenes for the show that did not take place where he sets them and/or involve characters that did not actually take part in those scenes (and often both). This is not to in any way criticize the historical accuracy of the material, but rather to recognize the difficulty in portraying historical events in an entertaining show (and you can only make so many sets and have so many characters - Miranda acknowledges in *Hamilton - The Revolution* that he deviates from what really happened where necessary for the show's content and flow). I have made a conscious decision to NOT point out historical inaccuracies, because the show could not possibly be better, so all liberties taken by Miranda were justified. If you want to get all the facts, buy and read Ron Chernow's biography, *Alexander Hamilton*, as Miranda did (and as I did) – a tremendous piece of work.

Given the above, I have tried my best to explain how each location is used in *Hamilton*, either as a setting for a scene in the show, as the location where an event portrayed in the show actually occurred, or if it was just mentioned (but is important). Hopefully, you will have the opportunity to see the show and can use this book as a resource to help you appreciate where all these events happened, or as a guide so that you can visit some of these locations and try to walk in the footsteps of the great men (and women) that helped shape our country.

Because Hamilton has been such a positive experience for me and my family, a portion of any profits from sales of this book will be donated to charity, mostly split between Graham Windham, the orphanage that Eliza Hamilton started (yes – it still exists!) and HeForShe, in part because the beat-box that Emma Watson did with Miranda was amazing (it's also a great cause, and my daughter loves Emma Watson).

 @wwtrwih

HOW THIS BOOK WORKS

I have tried to make this book as straightforward as possible, but a few things would benefit from explanation. I use a few different descriptions when referring to the songs and locations, with the following meanings:

- **Setting for** – this means the location is the stage setting in the show for the song;
- **Mentioned in** – this means the location is mentioned in the song, either by name or by referring to something that happened at the location;
- **Location for** – this means the events portrayed in the song happened in real life at the location (even though the stage setting may be different); this occurs most often where a song portrays events that happened in multiple locations at multiple times;
- **Who was *really* there?** – this refers to which historical figures from the show were ever at that location in real life (as best as I could determine based on research). This does not refer to who is portrayed in the show as being there, or to which characters sing any particular song – you can get that information from the *Hamilton* Broadway cast recording (which you own, of course);
- **Can you go there?** – this simply means whether the location stills exists in some form that might make it worth your while to see, or whether it has been built over in the ensuing years.

I would love any input, and if this book ends up seeing a lot of use I may prepare future updates or an expanded edition. Please send suggestions or comments (e.g., locations to add, thoughts re: connections to the Broadway show) to Info@wwtrwih.com, or tweet suggestions and include @wwtrwih. **Please also see page 80 for info on ordering the eBook or additional paperback books – they make great gifts and stocking stuffers.**

If you like this book, it would mean a lot to me if you would share it on social media on Facebook, Instagram, Twitter, etc. – please include @wwtrwih and #Hamilton.

ENJOY!

CHAPTER ONE

HAMILTON LOCATIONS
IN NEW YORK CITY

History is happening in Manhattan...

Alexander Hamilton was a New Yorker, so a lot of the events depicted in the show occurred in New York City (and I live in New York City), and this is the focus of this book (this book is primarily designed to be a guide for people in New York City to see all the locations related to *Hamilton: An American Musical* that are located in and near the city, and to provide historical information about those locations).

FRAUNCES TAVERN

| **Setting for**: | *Aaron Burr, Sir – Act I*
My Shot – Act I
The Story of Tonight – Act I
The Story of Tonight (Reprise) – Act I
Wait For It – Act I |

The tavern is the setting for Aaron Burr, Sir *and* My Shot *(from "Hamilton – The Revolution"), and while it is unclear whether the other songs listed above are also meant to be set in Fraunces Tavern, they each take place in a tavern with a similar set design.*

Who was *really* there?	Aaron Burr Alexander Hamilton George Washington
Location:	54 Pearl Street
Subway:	**1** South Ferry; **2** **3** Wall Street; **4** **5** Bowling Green; **J** **Z** Broad Street; **R** Whitehall Street/South Ferry
Can you go there?	Yes – it still exists as a national historic landmark, museum and restaurant. The restaurant is open 7 days a week from 11AM-2AM (you can book a table at www.frauncestavern.com or by calling 212-968-1776). The museum is open 12-5 M-F and 11-5 Sat/Sun. Don't miss the annual Fourth of July early morning walking tour (www.frauncestavernmuseum.org)!
Designations:	New York City Landmark (1965) National Register of Historic Places (2008)

History/Items of Interest:

The structure was built as a house by Etienne DeLancey in 1719 and then sold in 1762 to Samuel Fraunces, who converted it into a tavern named the Queen's Head.

The tavern served as the meeting place of the Sons of Liberty before the Revolution. The New York Chamber of Commerce was founded in 1768 at a meeting here, and the tavern hosted British-American Board of Inquiry meetings during the American Revolution. The tavern was the site of the dinner held on December 4, 1783 where *George Washington* bade farewell to his Continental Army officers. After the war, the departments of Foreign Affairs, War and Treasury of the Confederation Congress kept their offices here.

The Society of the Cincinnati met at the tavern at least once in the early 1800s – *Aaron Burr* and *Alexander Hamilton* attended. The building was destroyed by fires and rebuilt several times during the 19th century – the original design is unknown. The building passed between several owners and was finally scheduled for demolition in 1900. The Daughters of the American Revolution, among other groups, convinced the New York state government to designate the building as a park, thus saving the building until it was ultimately acquired by the Sons of the Revolution of New York in 1904. The building was "restored" soon thereafter, but without the original plans the restoration is thought to have involved substantial guesswork.

| **Setting for**: | *The Schuyler Sisters – Act I* |
| | *Farmer Refuted – Act I* |

Angelica, Eliza and Peggy work it downtown in the Common in The Schuyler Sisters, *and Alexander Hamilton takes on a pro-British speaker there in* Farmer Refuted.

Who was *really* there?	Aaron Burr
	Alexander Hamilton
	George Washington
Location:	City Hall Park, as this site is now known (bordered by Broadway, Chambers Street and Park Row).
Subway:	② ③ Park Place; ④ ⑤ ⑥ Brooklyn Bridge – City Hall; Ⓐ Ⓒ Ⓙ Ⓩ Chambers Street; Ⓡ City Hall
Can you go there?	Yes – City Hall Park is a great green space in Lower Manhattan that provides a place to relax and take a breath during your day. A stone circular tablet at the southern end of the park provides some history about the site. The park is open from 6AM to midnight.
Designations:	New York City Landmark (City Hall)
	National Register of Historic Places (City Hall)
	National Historic Landmark (City Hall)

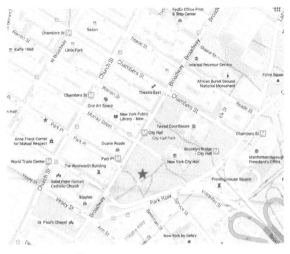

History/Items of Interest:

The park's western boundary was a Native American trail that later became Broadway. In 1765, New Yorkers protested the Stamp Act at the site, and a year later the first "Liberty Pole," a mast topped by a vane with the word "liberty," was built at the site (a replica stands between City Hall and Broadway, near its original location).

The Common was the site of *Alexander Hamilton*'s first major public speech, at a meeting of the Sons of Liberty on July 6, 1774, where he spoke in support of the Boston Tea Party and a boycott of British goods. When Hamilton (with others) stole cannons from Ft. George in The Battery on August 23, 1775, they brought the cannons to the Common. On July 9, 1776, *George Washington* read the Declaration of Independence to a crowd at the Common.

During the American Revolution, the British controlled New York and used the debtor's prison on the north end of the Common (where the Tweed Courthouse now stands) to hold prisoners, executing 250 of them on gallows behind the Soldiers' Barracks.

New Yorkers used the park for gatherings throughout the 19th century, including meetings after the declaration of the Mexican-American War in 1846, and a call to volunteers in 1862 to enlist in the Civil War (during the Civil War the park was used to house troops). After President Lincoln was assassinated, his funeral procession for New York residents began at City Hall.

The park is home to more than a dozen monuments and the Mould fountain in the center of the park. In 1991, during the construction of a nearby federal office building, an African burial ground was uncovered on portions of the northern part of the park.

THE BATTERY

East Coast Memorial in The Battery

Mentioned in:	*Right Hand Man – Act I*

Some of the battles mentioned in this song were fought at The Battery. This was also the location of Fort George, where Alexander Hamilton stole British cannons.

Who was *really* there?	Alexander Hamilton George Washington
Location:	Southern tip of Manhattan
Subway:	① South Ferry; ④ ⑤ Bowling Green Ⓡ Whitehall Street/South Ferry
Can you go there?	Yes and no – you can visit and walk around Battery Park (and catch a ferry to the Statue of Liberty or Ellis Island there), but you'll mainly be visiting a part of the city that didn't exist in the 1800s (see "History"). You can also visit the Alexander Hamilton U.S. Custom House, which sits where Fort George was located.
Designations:	New York City Landmark National Register of Historic Places

History/Items of Interest:

The southern tip of Manhattan has been known as The Battery since the Dutch settled the island and constructed Fort Amsterdam there in the 17th century to protect the city from approaches by sea.

Fort Amsterdam changed names several times (based upon the ruling country), including being named Fort George during the rule of George I, George II and George III. During the American Revolution, *George Washington*'s troops seized the fort from the British in 1775. Guns from the fort fired on the British during the Battle of Long Island. *Alexander Hamilton* (along with several of his fellow King's College students) stole cannons from Fort George on August 23, 1775. The British recaptured Fort George and ruled New York from the fort for the remainder of the Revolution. The colonists finally took back the fort on Evacuation Day on November 25, 1783 after the British left.

Fort George was torn down in 1790, and its materials were used as landfill for the area that became Battery Park. While Fort George had been located on the shoreline, the Alexander Hamilton U.S. Custom House (which sits where Fort George was located) is now several blocks from shore due to landfilling over the years.

The West Battery (now called Castle Clinton) was built in 1811 in The Battery when it was determined that fortifications in the area were still needed due to further conflicts with the British in the War of 1812. Castle Clinton was originally built on an island off the shore, but now sits within Battery Park due to landfilling.

Battery Park was renamed as The Battery by the New York City Department of Parks and the Battery Conservancy in 2015.

KING'S COLLEGE

College Hall at King's College, 1790

Mentioned in: *My Shot – Act I*
Blow Us All Away – Act II

Alexander Hamilton sings about getting a scholarship to King's College in My Shot, *and Philip Hamilton has just graduated from the college in* Blow Us All Away.

Who was *really* there?   Alexander Hamilton
Philip Hamilton

Location: King's College was bordered by present-day West Broadway, Murray Street, Barclay Street and Church Street.

Subway: Historic Site of King's College:
1 2 3 A C J Z Chambers Street
4 5 6 Brooklyn Bridge – City Hall
R City Hall

Columbia University:
1 116th St. – Columbia University

Can you go there?   No and yes. King's College is now known as Columbia College, the oldest undergraduate college at Columbia University, which is located on the Upper West Side in Manhattan – the main entrance is on Broadway at 116th Street. Groups of fewer than ten people can tour Columbia's Morningside campus on their own or join a guided tour at 1PM M-F (the Visitors Center is open 9-5 M-F; you can get a self-guided tour there, which tells you where to find statues of Hamilton and Thomas Jefferson).

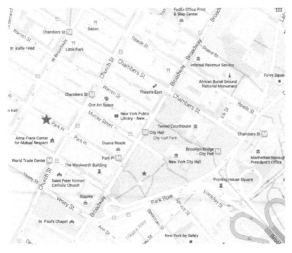

History/Items of Interest:

King's College was founded by royal charter of King George II and enrolled its first class in a room in Trinity Church in 1754. The land for the Park Place location (where *Alexander Hamilton* attended) was presented to the college by Trinity Church. John Jay (*Federalist Papers* author) also graduated from the college.

When the American Revolution began, the president was Myles Cooper (a royalist) – Cooper was threatened and ultimately chased back to England by a mob of patriots in May 1775. Hamilton held off the mob long enough for Cooper to escape by doing what he did best, launching into a speech (condemning the mob's conduct).

The campus was used as a military hospital during the war, first by the Continental Army and then by the British after they seized New York in late 1776 (until they vacated the city in 1783).

The college reopened in 1784 (largely due to the efforts of Hamilton and Jay) under a New York State charter as Columbia College. A charter from New York City in 1787 established Columbia College in its present form (and remains in force today, with slight amendments).

The college was renamed Columbia University in 1896, with the undergraduate school keeping the name Columbia College. The campus relocated to its current Upper West Side location in 1897.

Hamilton Hall is an academic building on the Columbia campus, and a statue of Alexander Hamilton stands outside the building entrance. Appropriately given its namesake, Hamilton Hall has been the site for much student protest activity over the years.

16

RICHMOND HILL

Location for: *Right Hand Man – Act I*
Your Obedient Servant – Act II

Aaron Burr met George Washington in Washington's office at Richmond Hill during the American Revolution, and this meeting occurs in Right Hand Man. *Burr later lived at Richmond Hill when he exchanged letters with Alexander Hamilton about their fateful duel as sung in* Your Obedient Servant.

Who was *really* there?

Aaron Burr
Alexander Hamilton
James Madison
George Washington

Location:

Present-day Varick Street, between Charlton Street and Vandam Street.

Subway:

❶ Houston Street
ⓒ ⓔ Spring Street

Can you go there?

Not really – you can visit the neighborhood where Richmond Hill was once located (a portion of which has been designated a landmark and a historic district), but the house itself no longer exists.

Designations:

New York City Landmark (1966)
National Register of Historic Places (1973)

History/Items of Interest:

Richmond Hill was built on a 26-acre parcel of land just south of modern-day Greenwich Village and served as the residence/office of several of the major names of Revolutionary America.

First was *George Washington* – Richmond Hill served as his headquarters from April 1776 until the British forced the retreat of the Continental Army in August 1776 (after the Battle of Long Island) – it was here that he met *Aaron Burr*. The British occupied the property for the remainder of the war.

Next was John Adams – he and Abigail Adams lived there during his tenure as vice president under Washington while the nation's capital was in New York City.

Finally, the property was purchased in 1794 by Burr, who lived there with his daughter, Theodosia. Burr used the mansion to entertain distinguished guests, including *James Madison*. Burr was living at Richmond Hill at the time of his duel with *Alexander Hamilton*. The property was ultimately seized by Burr's creditors and sold to John Jacob Astor, who developed the property into hundreds of individual lots (Burr actually mapped out the different lots during his ownership, but didn't have the capital to develop them). The house itself was moved and saw several different uses over the years until it was finally demolished in 1849.

A portion of the estate became what is now the Charlton-King-Vandam Historic District (encompassing most of Charlton Street, King Street and Vandam Street between Varick Street and Avenue of the Americas). The district was designated a New York City landmark in 1966 for its concentration of Federal-style row houses and Greek Revival houses.

18

JEFFERSON'S RESIDENCE

Plaza in front of 59 Maiden Lane

Setting for: *The Room Where It Happens – Act II*

Thomas Jefferson arranged "the meeting... the venue, the menu, the seating" at his residence on Maiden Lane, where he, Alexander Hamilton and James Madison reached a compromise regarding Hamilton's plan to have the federal government assume the debts of the individual states and the permanent location of the nation's capital.

Who was *really* there?   Alexander Hamilton
Thomas Jefferson
James Madison

Location: 57 Maiden Lane

Subway: **2** **3** **4** **5** Fulton Street
A **C** **J** **Z** Fulton Street
R Cortlandt Street

Can you go there?   No and yes. There is a lovely plaza in front of 59 Maiden Lane (57 Maiden Lane no longer exists) where you can relax for a bit during your day, and don't miss the plaque on the outer wall of the building (at the west end of the plaza) commemorating Jefferson's former residence.

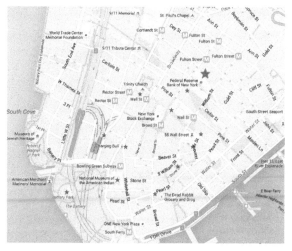

History/Items of Interest:

As recounted by **Thomas Jefferson** (then Secretary of State), **Alexander Hamilton** "basically begged me to join the fray" and to intervene in discussions and negotiations over Hamilton's Report on the Public Credit, which contained a provision that had the federal government assuming the debt of the individual states (and which had twice failed to pass the House of Representatives). Jefferson arranged a meeting among the two of them and **James Madison** (then a highly influential member of the House of Representatives) at Jefferson's residence on or about June 20, 1790. As an aside, Hamilton's Report is on display at the Museum of American Finance on Wall Street (in a room dedicated to Hamilton).

The result of the discussions among the three men was an agreement that Madison would not oppose the bill as strenuously when next brought before the House (by way of amendment from the Senate). In return, it was agreed that the nation's capital should be relocated from New York temporarily to Philadelphia (which was key in convincing the Pennsylvania delegation to go along with the bill) and then ultimately to its current location on the Potomac River. These compromises were borne out through the subsequent passage of the Assumption Bill and the Residence Act of 1790, giving Hamilton the ability to say "[I] got more than [I] gave, and I wanted what I got" (even though the compromise was not popular with many New Yorkers).

FEDERAL HALL

Setting for: *Non-Stop – Act I*
What'd I Miss – Act II
Cabinet Battle #1 – Act II

The murder trial of Levi Weeks, who was defended by Aaron Burr and Alexander Hamilton and which is mentioned in Non-Stop, *was held in City Hall. It was also the first U.S. Capitol Building and would have been the location for debates regarding Hamilton's debt plan in* Cabinet Battle #1, *and the initial meeting between Thomas Jefferson and James Madison when Jefferson first arrived in New York in* What'd I Miss *could have happened here.*

Who was *really* there?	Aaron Burr Alexander Hamilton Thomas Jefferson James Madison George Washington
Location:	26 Wall Street
Subway:	❶ Ⓡ Rector Street; ❷ ❸ ❹ ❺ Wall Street; Ⓙ Ⓩ Broad Street
Can you go there?	Yes – Federal Hall National Memorial (located on the site of the original Federal Hall) is open 9-5 M-F, and the National Park Service announced that the building would be open Saturdays for the summer of 2016. Admission is free.
Designations:	National Memorial (1955) National Register of Historic Places (1966) New York City Landmark (1965)

History/Items of Interest:

The original building was built in 1700 as New York's City Hall and housed the Continental Congress following the American Revolution (1785-1789). The building was enlarged and renamed Federal Hall when it became the nation's first Capitol under the new Constitution in 1789, and Congress held their initial meeting there on March 4, 1789. *George Washington* took his oath as the first U.S. president on the building's balcony on April 30, 1789.

Federal Hall initially housed all the branches of the government – the Senate, the House of Representatives (including *James Madison*), the Supreme Court and the Executive Branch offices (Washington and his cabinet, including *Thomas Jefferson*).

The National Park Service calls Federal Hall "the birthplace of American Government", and it lives up to this label. Federal Hall was the site of the Stamp Act Congress in 1765 (which claimed basic rights from *King George III*), and saw the proposal of the Bill of Rights, the drafting of a dozen Constitutional amendments, and the establishment of the U.S. federal court system.

After the government moved to Philadelphia in 1790, the building again housed the New York City government until it was razed in 1812. During this time, the building housed the courtroom where *Aaron Burr* and *Alexander Hamilton* defended their client Levi Weeks from a murder charge in 1800.

The current structure was built in 1842 as the first Customs House. It was designated as Federal Hall National Memorial in 1939. Congress convened in the building in September 2002 (the first time since 1790) to show support for New York following 9/11.

THE GRANGE

Setting for: *Blow Us All Away – Act II*
It's Quiet Uptown – Act II
Best of Wives and Best of Women – Act II
Who Lives, Who Dies, Who Tells Your Story
– Act II

The Hamiltons were living on the property where the Grange was to be located (the home was still under construction) when Philip Hamilton was killed in his duel – Alexander Hamilton speaks with Philip before his duel in Blow Us All Away, *and Hamilton and Eliza would have taken solace there as sung in* It's Quiet Uptown. *Eliza would have been at the Grange the morning of Hamilton's duel with Aaron Burr and would have spoken to him there in* Best of Wives and Best of Women. *Eliza lived at the Grange for a time after Hamilton's death while she started working on telling his story in* Who Lives, Who Dies, Who Tells Your Story.

Who was *really* there?	Alexander Hamilton Eliza Hamilton
Location:	414 West 141st Street in St. Nicholas Park
Subway:	① 137th Street – City College Ⓐ Ⓑ Ⓒ 135th Street
Can you go there?	Yes – Hamilton Grange National Memorial is operated by the National Park Service and has ranger-led tours. The memorial is open 9-5 W-Sun, and admission is free.
Designations:	National Memorial (1962) National Historic Landmark (1960) National Register of Historic Places (1966)

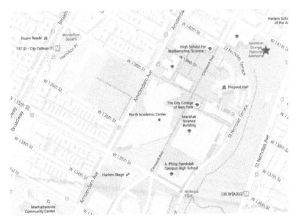

History/Items of Interest:

Alexander Hamilton bought the property that would eventually house the Grange in 1800, and the home was completed in 1802. Hamilton hired John McComb, Jr. as the architect for the home, and Ezra Weeks was the primary contractor (the brother of Levi Weeks, mentioned in *Non-Stop* as being the defendant in the murder trial with *Aaron Burr* and Hamilton as co-counsel).

Hamilton named it the Grange after his grandfather's estate in Scotland, and it was the only home ever owned by Hamilton (as well as the only residence of his that survives to this day). He lived there with *Eliza Hamilton* and the rest of his family. While *Philip Hamilton* lived on the property (the family lived in an existing building on the property while the Grange was being built), the home was completed after his death in the duel with George Eacker in November 1801. The home provided Hamilton with a retreat from the bustle on his downtown law practice to spend time with Eliza and their children, while also giving him and Eliza a place to host parties and socialize (including hosting a ball for 70+ guests just a couple of months before his duel with Burr).

After Eliza sold the property in 1833, the home was moved twice. It was acquired by St. Luke's Episcopal Church in the late 1800s and moved to present-day Convent Avenue. The American Scenic and Historic Preservation Society bought the building and turned it into a museum in 1924. It was transferred to the National Park Service and authorized as a National Memorial by Congress in 1962, and after a long period of disuse and then renovation (to restore the appearance to when Hamilton lived there) and relocation, the Grange was re-opened to the public in September 2011.

TRINITY CHURCH

Mentioned in: *Who Lives, Who Dies, Who Tells Your Story*
                     – Act II

Eliza Hamilton sings that Angelica Church is buried in Trinity Church near Alexander Hamilton.

Who was *really* there?	Aaron Burr	Alexander Hamilton
	Eliza Hamilton	Philip Hamilton
	Thomas Jefferson	James Madison
	Hercules Mulligan	Angelica Schuyler
	George Washington	

Location: 75 Broadway (Trinity Church); 74 Trinity Place (Trinity Church Cemetery)

Subway: ① Ⓡ Rector Street; ② ③ ④ ⑤ Wall Street; Ⓙ ② Broad Street

Can you go there? Yes – Trinity Church is an active Episcopal church with a full schedule of worship services Sun-F. The church is open to visitors every day 8-6, and the churchyard is open from 8-sunset every day.

Designations: New York City Landmark (1966)
                     National Historic Landmark (1976)
                     National Register of Historic Places (1976)

History/Items of Interest:

The charter for the parish was received on May 6, 1697 from the Royal Governor of New York. The first Trinity Church was built in 1698 as the first Anglican Church in Manhattan (the first rector was William Vesey). Trinity then built St. Paul's Chapel up Broadway in 1766 (to address Manhattan's exploding population).

The church was destroyed in the Great New York City Fire of 1776 (making St. Paul's the only remaining colonial-era church in Manhattan and the oldest public building in continuous use in the city). The New York State legislature ratified the church's charter in 1784. Services were held in St. Paul's Chapel until the second Trinity Church was constructed in 1790. After his inauguration as President in 1789, *George Washington* prayed in St. Paul's Chapel (members of the government, including *Alexander Hamilton* and John Jay, regularly worshipped here while the capital was in New York City). Hamilton's funeral procession on July 14, 1804 ended at Trinity Church, where he was eulogized by Gouverneur Morris and laid to rest.

The second church was torn down in 1839 (due to structural problems), and the third Trinity Church was built in 1846 – this is the current church. Trinity Church was the tallest building in New York until 1890 (when the New York World Building passed it). During the 9/11 attacks, the church acted as a refuge for people fleeing falling wreckage and debris.

Alexander Hamilton, *Eliza Hamilton*, *Philip Hamilton*, *Angelica Schuyler,* and *Hercules Mulligan* are all buried in the churchyard.

BAYARD'S MANSION

Location for: *The World Was Wide Enough – Act II*

Alexander Hamilton was taken here after his duel with Aaron Burr, and Angelica Schuyler and Eliza Hamilton "were both by his side as he died" here.

Who was *really* there?	Alexander Hamilton Eliza Hamilton Angelica Schuyler
Location:	80-82 Jane Street
Subway:	❶ ❷ ❸ Ⓐ Ⓒ Ⓔ 14ᵗʰ Street Ⓛ 8ᵗʰ Ave.
Can you go there?	Yes and no – the building pictured above is on the site of William Bayard's house, and there is a plaque on the wall of the building commemorating Hamilton's death.

History/Items of Interest:

William Bayard, Jr. was a prominent New York City banker and a close friend of *Alexander Hamilton* (he was a Bank of New York director). There is not much of note about the house itself other than as the site where Hamilton died.

After his duel with *Aaron Burr* the morning of July 11, 1804, Hamilton was rowed across the Hudson River to Bayard's dock and taken into his home. As word of the duel and Hamilton's mortal wound spread throughout the city, people congregated in front of Bayard's mansion. Bulletins providing updates on Hamilton's condition were circulated throughout the day.

Eliza Hamilton was summoned from the Grange to be by his side, and *Angelica Schuyler* joined her there. Hamilton was also attended there by doctors, several friends and clergy members. By all accounts, Hamilton was of clear mind and able to speak throughout the day.

The following day, all of Hamilton's children were brought into the room where he lay so that he could say goodbye to them. Hamilton's room was filled with friends and family throughout the day.

Hamilton died that day, July 12, 1804, in the early afternoon and more than a full day after the duel. A state funeral was held for him on July 14th, and after a procession through downtown New York City he was buried in the churchyard of Trinity Church.

Bit of trivia – some say that Bayard's mansion would have been located a block north of Jane Street, on present-day Horatio Street.

HAMILTON'S OTHER NEW YORK CITY RESIDENCES

26 Broadway, just opposite Broadway from Arturo Di Modica's *Charging Bull* statue

Location for: *Dear Theodosia – Act I*
Non-Stop – Act I
Schuyler Defeated – Act II
Hurricane – Act II
The Reynolds Pamphlet – Act II
Burn – Act II
Your Obedient Servant – Act II
Best of Wives and Best of Women – Act II

Each of these songs has Alexander Hamilton and/or Eliza Hamilton singing, and the context would indicate that at least a portion of the dialogue (or Hamilton's writing) would have taken place at his residence.

Who was *really* there? Alexander Hamilton
Eliza Hamilton
Philip Hamilton
Angelica Schuyler

Location: 57-58 Wall Street
26 Broadway
54 Cedar Street

Subway: **1** **R** Rector Street; **2** **3** **4** **5** Wall
Street; **J** **Z** Broad Street

Can you go there? No – none of these buildings remain, and there are no commemorative plaques relating to Hamilton at these locations.

History/Items of Interest:

<u>57-58 Wall Street</u>
Alexander Hamilton, *Eliza Hamilton* and *Philip Hamilton* lived here after the American Revolution, until the nation's capital was moved to Philadelphia in December 1790. Hamilton lived here when he wrote *The Federalist Papers* in 1787-1788.

<u>26 Broadway</u>
Hamilton, Eliza and Philip lived here after Hamilton resigned from his role as Treasury Secretary in January 1795.

<u>54 Cedar Street</u>
Hamilton had a townhouse here. He wrote his final note to Eliza and spent the night here before his fateful duel with *Aaron Burr*.

Liberty Plaza (where 54 Cedar Street would have been)

HAMILTON'S NEW YORK CITY OFFICES

Stone Street (stone-paved pedestrian street in Lower Manhattan)

Location for: *Non-Stop – Act I*
Election of 1800 – Act II
Your Obedient Servant – Act II

Each of these songs has Alexander Hamilton singing, and the context would indicate that at least a portion of the dialogue (or Hamilton's writing) would have taken place at his office.

Who was *really* there?   Alexander Hamilton
Eliza Hamilton

Location: 36 Greenwich Street
69 Stone Street
12 Garden Street (now Exchange Place)

Subway: ① ® Rector Street; ② ③ ④ ⑤ Wall Street; ⒥ ⓩ Broad Street

Can you go there?   No – none of these buildings remain, and there are no commemorative plaques at these locations.

Designations: New York City Landmark (1996) – Stone Street is protected as a Historic District

History/Items of Interest:

36 Greenwich Street

Alexander Hamilton worked out of this office during his time as general and second-in-command under *George Washington*, who was appointed to command a new American army in 1798. Washington delegated Hamilton the responsibility and authority to form the new army, which Hamilton did with his typical attention to minutiae with respect to all aspects of the army.

He continued to practice law out of this office, including during the Levi Weeks trial in 1800, when he acted as co-counsel for the defendant along with *Aaron Burr*.

69 Stone Street

Hamilton had his law office here at the time of *Philip Hamilton*'s duel with George Eacker, as well as when he was working on having the Grange built and the associated property landscaped. Stone Street is now a pedestrian street with lots of bars and restaurants and would be a good place for a rest during your visit and to "raise a glass to freedom" in Hamilton's memory.

12 Garden Street

This was Hamilton's final law office, and he spent his last days getting his affairs and those of his law clients in order before his duel with Aaron Burr. He was in this office when he received Burr's initial letter demanding an explanation for statements attributed to Hamilton.

CHAPTER TWO

OTHER NEW YORK CITY LOCATIONS
OF NOTE TO *HAMILTON*

...you're here with us in New York City

The following New York City locations are not particularly important with respect to the content of *Hamilton: An American Musical*, but they are of note with respect to the show itself.

MORRIS–JUMEL MANSION

Location for: *Right Hand Man – Act I*

George Washington and his men have "gotta run to Harlem quick" following the Battle of Long Island. He "runs" to Morris-Jumel Mansion, which serves as his temporary headquarters.

Who was *really* there?	Aaron Burr Alexander Hamilton Thomas Jefferson George Washington
Location:	Roger Morris Park, 65 Jumel Terrace
Subway:	① 157th Street ⓒ 163rd Street Ⓑ Ⓓ 155th Street
Can you go there?	Yes – the building is operated as a museum and is open from 10-4 T-F and from 10-5 Sat/Sun (though it is closed some holidays). There is an admission fee for the museum, and there are guided tours (for an additional fee; www.morrisjumel.org or 212-923-8008 for reservations).
Designations:	New York City Landmark (1967/1975) National Historic Landmark (1961) National Register of Historic Places (1966)

History/Items of Interest:

The Morris-Jumel Mansion was built in 1765 by Colonel Roger Morris, and the estate was named "Mount Morris". Mount Morris was one of the highest points in Manhattan, with clear views of New Jersey, Connecticut, and all of New York harbor (which was to make it a strategic military location).

The Morrises had to leave their home during the American Revolution due to their Tory sympathies. Following the Battle of Long Island, *George Washington* made the house his headquarters from September 14 to October 21 of 1776. From this strategic position, he planned his army's first successful victory – The Battle of Harlem Heights (though the Continental Army was soon forced to leave Manhattan by the British). After Washington's army abandoned Manhattan Island, the house served as headquarters to the British. After the war, the property was confiscated by the U.S. government and then purchased by Stephen Jumel in 1810, who lived there with his wife, Eliza Bowen.

After Jumel died in 1832, Eliza married *Aaron Burr*, though the marriage was short-lived and Eliza filed for divorce in 1833. Eliza lived in the house until her death in 1865. In 1904, the city of New York purchased the house and turned it into a museum.

Today, the Morris-Jumel Mansion is the oldest remaining house in Manhattan and is a museum highlighting over 200 years of New York history, art, and culture.

Lin-Manuel Miranda was granted a writing space at the mansion, and he wrote a portion of *Hamilton* during his time there.

Location for:	*Greatest Show on Earth*
Who was there?	Everyone, (almost) every night
Location:	226 West 46th Street
Subway:	❶ 50th Street
	❶ ❷ ❸ ❼ Times Square – 42nd Street
	Ⓝ Ⓠ Ⓡ Ⓢ Times Square – 42nd Street
	Ⓐ Ⓒ Ⓔ 42nd Street – Port Authority
Can you go there?	Good luck getting tickets, and don't forget about the online lottery (see details at hamiltonbroadway.com). In August 2016, they stopped doing the Ham4Ham live performances at the theatre prior to the Wednesday matinee shows (but follow @HamiltonMusical on Twitter for updates; they may decide to do them again – it was a great way to see cast members perform live).

History/Items of Interest:

The Richard Rodgers Theatre opened in 1924 as the 46th Street Theatre, and it was renamed in 1990 to honor the composer Richard Rodgers.

The most important part of history for the Richard Rodgers Theatre (at least for the readers of this book) is of course being the Broadway venue of *Hamilton: An American Musical*. The show opened at the theatre on August 6, 2015, after a hugely successful run at the Public Theater and has set the box office record for the Richard Rodgers Theatre. The theatre is also the site of the #Ham4Ham live show, which takes place outside the theatre during the Wednesday matinee live lottery and features cast members and special guests (which are often performers from other Broadway shows).

The Richard Rodgers Theatre already had a history of successful shows before *Hamilton* arrived. The theatre currently holds the distinction of having housed the greatest number (eleven) of Tony Award-winning Best Plays and Best Musicals (including *Hamilton*, after its 2016 Tony Best Musical win), more than any other theatre on Broadway. Also on this list is *Lin-Manuel Miranda*'s first Broadway show, *In The Heights*, which won the 2008 Tony Award for Best Musical, as well as Tony winners *Guys and Dolls* (1951) and *Damn Yankees* (1956), and the theatre was also the venue for the *Chicago* revival when it won the 1997 Tony Award for Best Revival of a Musical.

CHAPTER THREE

OTHER ALEXANDER HAMILTON RELATED THINGS TO SEE AND DO IN NEW YORK CITY

... we just happen to be in the greatest city in the world

There are a lot of other places in the city that someone interested in Alexander Hamilton's life may be interested in visiting, even though they don't have any real connection with *Hamilton: An American Musical.* Some of them are listed in the following pages.

MUSEUM OF AMERICAN FINANCE

Location: 48 Wall Street

Subway: **1** **R** Rector Street

2 **3** **4** **5** Wall Street

J **Z** Broad Street

Visitor Info: The museum is open 10-4 T-Sat, and there is an admission fee for the museum (kids under 6 are free) – see www.moaf.org for more info.

Why go there? There is a room dedicated to Alexander Hamilton (Hamilton's Legacy) containing various Hamilton artifacts (e.g., his debt assumption report and a reproduction set of the pistols from his duel with Aaron Burr). And don't skip the museum shop, where you can pick up an Alexander Hamilton tie or bobblehead.

NEW-YORK HISTORICAL SOCIETY

Location:	170 Central Park West (at 77th Street)
Subway:	① 79th Street; ② ③ 72nd Street; ⑧ ⓒ 81st St – Museum of Natural History
Visitor Info:	The museum is open 10-6 T-Th and Sat, 10-8 F and 11-5 Sun, and there is an admission fee for the museum (kids under 5 are free) – see www.nyhistory.org for more info.
Why go there?	The museum has several Hamilton-related artifacts in its regular collection, and they host Hamilton-themed exhibits from time to time. The museum commemorated the bicentennial of Hamilton's death in 2004/5 with the exhibit "Alexander Hamilton: The Man Who Made Modern America", and the museum's 2016 "Summer of Hamilton" celebrated all things Hamilton in recognition of the success of *Hamilton: An American Musical* and Ron Chernow's biography (in addition to exhibiting artifacts from outside the museum's collection, the museum held special exhibitions and events).

COS CLOTHING STORE

Location: 129 Spring Street

Subway:

6 Spring Street
N **R** Prince Street
C **E** Spring Street

Visitor Info: The store is open 10-8 M-Sat and 11-7 Sun.

Why go there? This one's a bit out there. In the basement of the store is the 200+-year old "haunted" well involved in the Levi Weeks murder case (where Alexander Hamilton and Aaron Burr served as defense counsels for Weeks). The woman Weeks was accused of murdering was found in this well, and there have been reports of strange happenings around the well over the years.

MUSEUM OF THE CITY OF NEW YORK

Location: 1220 Fifth Avenue (at 103rd Street)

Subway: **1** 79th Street

                     2 **3** 72nd Street

                     B **C** 81st St – Museum of Natural History

Visitor Info: The museum is open 10-6 every day, and there is an admission fee for the museum (ages 19 and under are free) – see www.mcny.org for more info.

Why go there?   The museum has a permanent collection of portraits of many Revolution-era people, including Alexander Hamilton and George Washington, and the museum had a special portrait exhibit in 2016 that featured these portraits (call the museum at 212-534-1672 for info on current exhibits). Don't miss the statue of Hamilton outside the museum (near the corner of 104th Street), and don't forget to look at the museum shop's Hamilton-related prints.

CHAPTER FOUR

HAMILTON LOCATIONS
IN NEW JERSEY

Everything is legal in New Jersey

Many of the events depicted in the show occurred in New Jersey (mainly during the American Revolution, as George Washington and his troops camped in New Jersey for several periods during the war). While the focus of this book is New York City, the more adventurous of you may be willing to venture over to New Jersey to see some of the locations that are of particular importance to the life of Alexander Hamilton and the content of *Hamilton: An American Musical.*

WEEHAWKEN, NEW JERSEY

Setting for: *Blow Us All Away – Act II*
Stay Alive (Reprise) – Act II
The World Was Wide Enough – Act II

The fateful duel between Philip Hamilton and George Eacker happens in Blow Us All Away. *Philip sings that he "was aiming for the sky" in recounting the duel to Alexander Hamilton in* Stay Alive (Reprise). *The duel between Aaron Burr and Alexander Hamilton, where Hamilton was mortally wounded, also occurs here in* The World Was Wide Enough.

Who was *really* there?	Aaron Burr Alexander Hamilton Philip Hamilton
Location:	South of Hamilton Park (at JFK Boulevard East and Hamilton Avenue)
Subway/Bus:	**1** **2** **3** **7** Times Square – 42nd Street **N** **Q** **R** **S** Times Square – 42nd Street **A** **C** **E** 42nd Street – Port Authority
	From Port Authority, take NJ Transit bus 165, 166 or 168 to Hamilton Park, Boulevard East at Bonn Place (20 minutes).
Can you go there?	Yes – you can visit Hamilton Park for an unobstructed view of the Manhattan skyline. You can also see the Hamilton Monument and plaques commemorating the Hamilton-Burr duel along Hamilton Avenue (just south of Hamilton Park).

History/Items of Interest:

Philip Hamilton

The duel between *Philip Hamilton* and George I. Eacker occurred on November 23, 1801 at what is now Weehawken, NJ. Eacker, a Republican lawyer, gave a speech at a 4th of July celebration that year, during which he "disparaged [Philip's] father's legacy in front of a crowd". At some point Philip saw the speech and the references to Hamilton. Philip encountered Eacker several months later, at the Park Theater in lower Manhattan, and he and a friend confronted Eacker about the speech, which quickly led to duel challenges from both of the men, each of which Eacker accepted.

The duel between Philip's friend and Eacker occurred first, ending with four missed shots. Attempts to negotiate a truce for Philip failed, leading to the duel in Weehawken (since "everything is legal in New Jersey") the next day. Hamilton advised Philip to reserve his fire, and Eacker mortally wounded Philip with his first shot. Philip was taken to the home of John and Angelica Church, where he died the following day (with both parents at his side).

Alexander Hamilton

The much more famous duel between *Alexander Hamilton* and *Aaron Burr* occurred on July 11, 1804 on the same site in Weehawken. Contrasting Philip's duel, which occurred three days after he confronted Eacker, Alexander's duel with Burr was long in the making. The two men shared a lifetime of disagreements and contention, primarily concerning politics, and politics was at the heart of the matter that finally pushed Burr to challenge Hamilton.

Hamilton had opposed Burr's campaign to become governor of New York in 1804 (which Burr lost). In June 1804, Burr learned of injurious statements Hamilton had allegedly made about Burr, which given his recent political defeat were the last straw. On June 18th, Burr and William Van Ness met at Richmond Hill, and Van Ness delivered a letter to Hamilton at his Garden Street office that day demanding an explanation of Hamilton's statements. The two men exchanged several letters to no avail, and Van Ness delivered a formal duel request to Nathaniel Pendleton (for Hamilton) on June 27th. The duel was set for July 11th so that Hamilton could attend to his law practice and put his affairs in order. He spent the night before the duel at his Cedar Street townhouse.

As he had advised Philip, Hamilton decided to "throw away his shot" and reserve his fire. And as it had for Philip, this decision proved fatal, as Burr's first shot mortally wounded Hamilton (like Philip, Hamilton was shot above his right hip). He was taken to the home of William Bayard, where he died the following day, July 12th, and where "Angelica and Eliza were both at his side when he died". He was buried in the churchyard at Trinity Church on July 14th, after a funeral procession through lower Manhattan.

MORRISTOWN, NEW JERSEY

Ford Mansion

Setting for: *Right Hand Man – Act I*
A Winter's Ball – Act I
Helpless – Act I
Satisfied – Act I

George Washington invited Alexander Hamilton to be his aide-de-camp in Morristown in 1777, as sung in Right Hand Man. *Washington used Ford Mansion as his headquarters during much of the winter of 1779/1780; Hamilton also lived here and attended nearby dances, such as the one sung about in* A Winter's Ball, Helpless *and* Satisfied. *Eliza Schuyler lived at the Schuyler-Hamilton House during that winter, and much of Hamilton's courtship of her as sung in* Helpless *happened here.*

Who was *really* there?   Alexander Hamilton
Eliza Hamilton
Philip Schuyler
George Washington

Location: Ford Mansion – 230 Morris Avenue
Schuyler-Hamilton House – 5 Olyphant Pl.

Subway/Train: **1** **2** **3** **A** **C** **E** 34th St. – Penn Station

From Penn Station, take New Jersey Transit (Morris & Essex Line) to Morristown.

Can you go there?   Yes – you can visit Ford Mansion (which is part of Morristown National Historic Park) W-Sun from 9:30-5, and there are tours of the mansion (first-come, first served). The Schuyler-Hamilton House is open Sundays from 2-4 (tours can be arranged) – call (973) 539-7502 for more info.

History/Items of Interest:

Ford Mansion

The winter of 1779/1780 was worse than the famous winter in Valley Forge (it remains the only time in recorded history that the waters around New York City froze over). *George Washington* used the mansion of Judy and Jacob Ford in Morristown as his headquarters that year. *Alexander Hamilton* also stayed in the mansion. However, the winter may have contributed to the social scene at the mansion, as Washington hosted dinners and receptions there that attracted guests, including young women, as an escape from the harsh weather – Hamilton was a regular attendee at these events. During this winter Washington and his officers attended nearby balls, which may have been frequented by *Eliza Schuyler*.

Schuyler-Hamilton House

During the winter of 1779/1780, Eliza's aunt, together with her husband, Dr. John Cochran (surgeon general of the Continental Army), stayed at the home of Dr. Jabez Campfield. Eliza arrived in Morristown in February 1780 and stayed with the Cochrans for the winter. Having already met Eliza in Albany, Hamilton began to socialize with Eliza soon thereafter. Hamilton used his vast intellect, charm and writing abilities to court Eliza, and she was helpless to resist – they decided to get married little more than a month after Eliza's arrival. Eliza's father, *Philip Schuyler* arrived in Morristown in April and likely visited the house (though he and his wife resided elsewhere while in Morristown).

The house was purchased by the Morristown chapter of the New Jersey Daughters of the American Revolution in 1923 and renamed in honor of Eliza Schuyler and Alexander Hamilton.

The Green

The Morristown Green now has the feel of a neighborhood park, but at one time it was a hub of military activity during Washington's first winter in Morristown with his Continental Army in 1777. It was here at Jacob Arnold's Tavern, on January 20, 1777, that Washington invited Hamilton to join his staff as an aide-de-camp (advancing Hamilton to the rank of lieutenant colonel upon his official appointment on March 1, 1777) – a plaque marks the original location of the tavern. Fans of the show may also want to visit the park to see the group of life-size statues of Washington, Hamilton and the *Marquis de Lafayette* (depicting Lafayette informing Washington and Hamilton on May 10, 1780 that the French would be coming to support the Americans in their fight against the British).

The Green is located approximately one mile due west of the Ford Mansion (you can reach it by going along Lafayette Avenue).

BATTLE OF MONMOUTH – NEW JERSEY

Setting for: *Stay Alive – Act I*

George Washington and his Continental Army snatched "a stalemate from the jaws of defeat" here.

Who was *really* there?	Aaron Burr Alexander Hamilton Marquis de Lafayette John Laurens Charles Lee George Washington
Location:	Border of Freehold Township/Manalapan Township
Getting there:	You pretty much have to drive to get there.
Can you go there?	Yes – Monmouth Battlefield State Park preserves the historical battlefield where this battle was fought. The park is open daily from 8AM-6PM during Fall/Spring, from 8AM-4:30PM during Winter and from 8AM-8PM during Summer (the Visitor Center is open 9AM-4PM daily). There is an annual reenactment of the 1778 Battle of Monmouth at the park in late June (check out www.njparksandforests.org for info).
Designations:	New Jersey Register of Historic Places (1971) National Historic Landmark District (1961) National Register of Historic Places (1966)

History/Items of Interest:

The opportunity for this battle arose when the British army under General Henry Clinton decided in June 1778 to evacuate Philadelphia and retreat to New York (which required that they cross New Jersey). *George Washington* recognized that the retreating British army could be vulnerable to attack during their slow move across New Jersey. Despite reservations from his war council, Washington decided to attack if the opportunity presented itself. General *Charles Lee* initially refused to serve as Washington's second in command and only relented after Washington assigned the position to the *Marquis de Lafayette*.

Lee was ordered to attack the British, who were camped near Monmouth Court House in Freehold, NJ, the morning of June 28, 1778 (*Alexander Hamilton* drafted Washington's order). Washington would bring up the rear with the main force of the army.

While Lee did in fact attack the rear guard of the British army (under General Cornwallis), Washington arrived to find Lee's troops in full retreat. Washington took command of Lee's men and rallied them to hold off the British until the main force was able to arrive (Washington had ridden ahead after receiving word of Lee's retreat).

The heat of the day added to the stress of battle, as Washington's white charger died from the heat (forcing him to take up a new horse). Hamilton, *John Laurens* and *Aaron Burr* all had their horses shot from under them, and Burr was stricken with sunstroke that ended his combat duty for the rest of the war.

The battle is considered to have essentially been a draw (as the British were able to continue their retreat), but it served to truly cement Washington as a war hero and skilled commander, and it established Hamilton as courageous and unflappable in battle. Lee was arrested for disobeying orders and eventually subjected to a court martial (which led to his suspension from the army for one year). Lee spoke out regularly against Washington (and, to a lesser extent, Hamilton), ultimately leading to Laurens challenging Lee to a dual that occurred outside of Philadelphia on December 23, 1778, as sung in *Ten Duel Commandments* (with Hamilton serving as Laurens' second).

Of note is that the legend of "Molly Pitcher" is associated with this battle. One version has Mary Ludwig Hays, the wife of a local American artilleryman, bringing water for the crews and cannons and taking her husband's place in the battle after he died. Look for markings on the battlefield of "Molly Pitcher's Spring".

ELIZABETHTOWN, NEW JERSEY

The Snyder Academy of Elizabethtown

Setting for: *Aaron Burr, Sir – Act I*

Even though the lead-in to Aaron Burr, Sir *says "1776 – New York City", both Alexander Hamilton and Aaron Burr had similar contacts in Elizabethtown (now split into Elizabeth and Union) during 1773 and may have had their initial meeting there.*

Who was *really* there?	Aaron Burr Alexander Hamilton Marquis de Lafayette George Washington
Location:	Snyder Academy – 42 Broad St., Elizabeth Boxwood Hall – 1073 East Jersey St., Elizabeth Liberty Hall – 1003 Morris Avenue, Union
Subway/Train:	① ② ③ Ⓐ Ⓒ Ⓔ 34th St. – Penn Station From Penn Station, take New Jersey Transit (New Jersey Coast or Northeast Corridor Lines) to Elizabeth.
Can you go there?	Yes – Snyder Academy has a small museum room and offers campus tours – both typically require appointments (call (908) 353-2131 to make arrangements). Boxwood Hall is open M-F from 9-noon and 1-5 (call (908) 282-7617 to confirm hours). Liberty Hall Museum is open M-Sat from 10-4 from April-December (there is an admission fee – call (908) 527-0400 for more info).

History/Items of Interest:

The Snyder Academy of Elizabethtown

Through letters of introduction provided by Rev. Hugh Knox, shortly after arriving in New York *Alexander Hamilton* found his way to the Elizabethtown Academy, where he would complete his college preparatory studies. He was following in the footsteps of *Aaron Burr*, who attended the school several years earlier, and his first meeting with Burr may have occurred during Hamilton's time in Elizabethtown. The school's headmaster, Francis Barber, would later fight in the Battle of Yorktown, serving under Hamilton.

Boxwood Hall

Through another of Knox's letters, Hamilton was introduced to Elias Boudinot and became a frequent visitor to Boxwood Hall, Boudinot's home, during his time in Elizabethtown. *George Washington* had lunch here in April 1789, before heading to New York for his inauguration. During his return visit to the States in 1824, the *Marquis de Lafayette* spent the night at Boxwood Hall.

Liberty Hall

Yet another Knox letter introduced Hamilton to William Livingston, and Hamilton lived with Livingston and his family during at least part of his time in Elizabethtown (though likely in temporary housing during the construction of Liberty Hall). In addition to introducing Hamilton to society (and possibly influencing Hamilton's political views), Livingston and his family would play many roles in Hamilton's life.

Livingston's son Brockholst was co-counsel with Hamilton and Burr during the Levi Weeks trial. Livingston's brother-in-law, Lord Stirling, was the first to approach Hamilton to be his military aide, in 1776 (Hamilton declined), and he would later command his vastly outnumbered troops in the Battle of Brooklyn, fighting long enough to allow Washington to ferry most of his forces across the East River. Lord Stirling briefly commanded Hamilton's artillery company (before Hamilton became Washington's aide-de-camp) and even presided over Charles Lee's court martial (at which Hamilton was a witness against Lee; Burr, by contrast, submitted a letter defending Lee). John Jay, co-author of *The Federalist Papers*, was Livingston's son-in-law. Finally, Livingston's daughter Kitty was an early recipient of Hamilton's amorous attentions, and she may have played a key role in bringing Hamilton and Eliza Schuyler together, as she was a friend of both.

Liberty Hall Museum is 1-1/2 miles northwest of the other two sites. You can reach it by going along Morris Ave., and there are two buses (26/52) that get you most of the way there (and back). Visit the Alexander Hamilton room, where he was often a guest.

PATERSON, NEW JERSEY

Mentioned in: *Take A Break – Act II*
Say No to This - Act II

While Take A Break *follows* Cabinet Battle #1 *(about Alexander Hamilton's debt plan), Hamilton was actually working on his* Report on Manufactures *during 1791 (when Eliza Hamilton takes the kids to "all go stay with [her] father" in Albany) - this report led to the establishment of Paterson as the nation's first industrial city. Hamilton is "someone under stress" in* Say No to This *due to his work on the report and his efforts to establish Paterson.*

Who was *really* there?	Alexander Hamilton Marquis de Lafayette George Washington
Location:	Paterson Great Falls National Historical Park - 72 McBride Avenue, Paterson
Subway/Bus:	❶ ❷ ❸ ❼ Times Square – 42nd Street Ⓝ Ⓠ Ⓡ Ⓢ Times Square – 42nd Street Ⓐ Ⓒ Ⓔ 42nd Street – Port Authority From Port Authority, take NJ Transit bus 161 or 190 to Market Street (45 minutes).
Can you go there?	Yes – Paterson Great Falls National Historical Park is operated by the National Park Service and has ranger-led tours and a Welcome Center. Call 862-257-3709, or visit www.hamiltonpartnership.org or www.nps.gov/pagr, for more info.

History/Items of Interest:

Alexander Hamilton, *George Washington* and the *Marquis de Lafayette* visited the Great Falls of the Passaic River on July 10, 1778, shortly after the Battle of Monmouth. While there they enjoyed a brief break from war and a picnic lunch of ham, tongue, "excellent" biscuits and grog. Washington and Hamilton would return to Great Falls during the Revolutionary War in 1780, and Lafayette visited Great Falls during his visit to the States in 1824.

Like so many other locations with a connection to Hamilton, the Great Falls would reappear in a later episode of his life. Hamilton submitted his *Report on Manufactures* to Congress in December 1791, in which he advocated the development of American industry as necessary to reduce reliance on foreign powers and to gain economic independence for the country. The report was nearly two years in the making, during which time Hamilton was laying the groundwork for its success. Hamilton began to acquire British manufacturing knowledge in 1790-91, and he was instrumental in the creation in late 1791 of the Society for the Establishment of Useful Manufactures (S.U.M.). The S.U.M. was the first corporation in New Jersey and was chartered to promote manufacturing by providing land, mill buildings and water power.

In typical Hamiltonian fashion, Hamilton was involved in almost all aspects of the project. He helped support the S.U.M.'s initial stock offering to secure necessary funding, he initiated the search for an appropriate site for such a town and he selected Pierre L'Enfant (fresh off his role as planner for the new federal capital that would later become Washington, D.C.) as town planner. While Hamilton may have remembered the Great Falls of the Passaic from his wartime visits, it was the power of the river and the 77-foot tall, 300-foot wide Great Falls that led him to select it as the site for the world's first city planned for industry. The charter (written mostly by Hamilton) for the new town of Paterson around the Great Falls was granted on November 22, 1791 – the town was named for New Jersey Governor William Paterson.

After initially losing money (which Hamilton, encouraging "Perseverance", had predicted), the S.U.M. became successful and remained so for 150 years, and Paterson manufactured the first Colt revolvers, silk, locomotives, the first submarines, aircraft engines and many of the goods Hamilton listed in his *Report on Manufactures*. Hamilton's report also noted that manufacturing would promote immigration, which he favored as a means to bring a "diversity of talents" to the country and because, as Hamilton would say (and prove), "Immigrants. We get the job done."

In recognition of the importance of Paterson as the realization of Hamilton's vision for an industrial America, legislation creating the Paterson Great Falls National Historical Park was signed by President Obama in 2009, and the park was established in 2011.

CHAPTER FIVE

HAMILTON LOCATIONS
FURTHER AFIELD

The world was wide enough...

Many of the events depicted in the show occurred outside of New York City and New Jersey. While the focus of this book is New York City, some of these non-NYC locations are of particular importance to the life of Alexander Hamilton and the content of *Hamilton: An American Musical*, so they are discussed in this book. However, detailed information about these sites (including specific locations and historical information) is beyond the scope of this book. Maybe we will cover these in a subsequent edition...

PHILADELPHIA, PENNSYLVANIA

First Bank of the United States

Location for:
Ten Duel Commandments – Act I
Meet Me Inside – Act I
Take a Break – Act II
Say No To This – Act II
Cabinet Battle #2 – Act II
Washington On Your Side – Act II
One Last Time – Act II
The Adams Administration – Act II
We Know – Act II
Hurricane – Act II
The Reynolds Pamphlet – Act II

Who was *really* there?
Aaron Burr
Alexander Hamilton
Thomas Jefferson
Charles Lee
James Madison
James Reynolds
Maria Reynolds
Eliza Hamilton
George Washington

Subway/Train: ❶ ❷ ❸ Ⓐ Ⓒ Ⓔ 34th St. – Penn Station
From Penn Station, take Amtrak or New Jersey Transit/SEPTA to Philadelphia.

Subway/Bus: ❶ ❷ ❸ ❼ Ⓝ Ⓠ Ⓡ Ⓢ Times Sq. – 42nd St.; Ⓐ Ⓒ Ⓔ 42nd St. – Port Authority
From Port Authority, there are several bus options to Philadelphia.

History/Items of Interest:

Even though the event that eventually led to the duel between *John Laurens* (with *Alexander Hamilton* as his second) and *Charles Lee* was the Battle of Monmouth, the duel took place several months later in a wood outside Philadelphia, so the events sung about in *Ten Duel Commandments* and the confrontation with *George Washington* in *Meet Me Inside* would have happened here.

Philadelphia became the temporary site of the nation's capital following the passing of the Residence Bill of 1790, and the government was relocated from New York City to Philadelphia in late 1790. Alexander Hamilton and *Eliza Hamilton* lived in Philadelphia during his remaining tenure as Treasury Secretary until his resignation in January 1795 (following which they returned to New York City).

All the events relating to the government during this time would have occurred in Philadelphia, including those sung about in *Cabinet Battle #2* (the battle between Hamilton and *Thomas Jefferson*), *Washington On Your Side*, *One Last Time*, and *The Adams Administration*.

The affair between Hamilton and *Maria Reynolds* happened during his time living in Philadelphia. As recounted in *Say No To This*, Maria sought assistance from Hamilton during the summer of 1791, and his initial offers of monetary aid transformed when it became "apparent that other than pecuniary consolation would be acceptable". The affair escalated from there when Eliza left for Albany without Hamilton, as he would not *Take a Break*. Hamilton's letter from and subsequent encounters with *James Reynolds*, also sung in *Say No To This*, took place in December 1791, leading to the payments from Hamilton to Reynolds.

The affair was to come back to haunt Hamilton when Reynolds was prosecuted for defrauding the U.S. government in 1792, resulting in a connection being made between Reynolds and Hamilton and eventually leading to the confrontation on December 15, 1792, sung about in *We Know*, where Hamilton was forced to defend his professional honor by revealing his affair with Maria.

It was several years before the charges against Hamilton of speculation with Reynolds arose again, through published attacks. Against the advice of his friends, Hamilton decided, as sung about in *Hurricane*, to write and publish *The Reynolds Pamphlet* in 1797 to address the charges. Even though Hamilton was living in New York City at the time, he returned to Philadelphia to write the pamphlet.

NEVIS AND ST. CROIX

Setting for: *Alexander Hamilton – Act I*

Alexander Hamilton was born on the island of Nevis on January 11, 1757. In the spring of 1765, Hamilton and his family relocated to St. Croix, where the events sung about Hamilton's work in the trading charter in Alexander Hamilton *occurred. He left St. Croix for New York City via a ship bound for Boston in the fall of 1772.*

Who was *really* there?   Alexander Hamilton

YORKTOWN, VIRGINIA

Setting for: *Yorktown (The World Turned Upside Down) – Act I*

The Battle of Yorktown was where Alexander Hamilton joined up with the Marquis de Lafayette for his last chance at combat and ordered his soldiers to take their bullets out of their guns – What!?! The Americans won the battle and the war essentially ended upon General Cornwallis' surrender, sending a young man to "frantically wave a white handkerchief".

Who was *really* there?
Alexander Hamilton
Marquis de Lafayette
John Laurens
George Washington

CHARLESTON, SOUTH CAROLINA

Setting for:
No song from the cast recording, but there is a scene in the show depicting when ***Alexander Hamilton*** learns of the death of ***John Laurens***. Even though the British had surrendered at Yorktown in 1781, the British still held several cities in the South, including Charleston, South Carolina. In late August 1782, Laurens attacked a British foraging expedition outside of Charleston and was shot and killed in what is known as the Battle of the Combahee River, becoming one of the last casualties of the American Revolution.

ALBANY, NEW YORK

Setting for: *Satisfied – Act I*

The wedding between Alexander Hamilton and Eliza Hamilton, which is part of the scene for Satisfied, *took place in Albany on December 14, 1780 at the estate of Philip Schuyler, the Pastures (now known as Schuyler Mansion).*

Mentioned in: *Take A Break – Act II*

Eliza wanted them to "go stay with [her] father" in Take A Break. *Angelica Schuyler also could not convince Hamilton to join them upstate, despite coming all the way from England.*

Who was *really* there?
Alexander Hamilton
Eliza Hamilton
Philip Hamilton
Angelica Schuyler
Philip Schuyler
Peggy Schuyler

ENGLAND

Setting for: *You'll Be Back – Act II*
What Comes Next – Act II
I Know Him – Act II

King George III viewed the American Revolution from afar as sung in these three songs. In addition to the war, King George III had to deal with unrest in London when "the price of this war" became more than his people were willing to pay. He met John Adams, as he sings in I Know Him, *when Adams was appointed American Minister to London in 1785.*

Mentioned in: *Take A Break – Act II*

Angelica Schuyler arrives from London and tries to convince Hamilton to go to Albany with her and Eliza in Take A Break.

Who was *really* there?
Aaron Burr
Alexander Hamilton
King George III
Thomas Jefferson
James Madison
Angelica Schuyler
George Washington

CHAPTER SIX

SUGGESTED ITINERARIES

Look around, look around...

Now that you know where everything is, you need to figure out what you really want to see and whether you have time to see it. I have included some suggestions on the following pages, organized by the amount of time required (Half-Day or Full-Day+). I have also included a couple of themed itineraries.

If you are planning your trip far enough in advance, you should think about booking a tour with Jimmy Napoli, who is a rock star when it comes to talking about Alexander Hamilton's life in New York City (he's been giving Hamilton tours for 20 years) – he has a couple of different tours and you can book him through hamiltonsnewyork.com.

Downtown

A great place to start is (1) **Trinity Church** (page 25), where you can visit Alexander Hamilton's grave, as well as those of Eliza Hamilton and some others. A short walk down Wall Street from there takes you to (2) **Federal Hall** (page 21), and further down the block is (3) the **Museum of American Finance** (page 41), where you can see replicas of the Hamilton-Burr duel pistols and other Hamilton-related items (and where you can pick up a Hamilton tie in the gift shop). If you have time for lunch or a drink, you can head to (4) **Stone Street** (page 31), which has several restaurants, or (5) **Fraunces Tavern** (page 9). If you don't, you can walk the half-mile to (7) **the Common** (page 11) for a beautiful green spot to take a break (don't miss the stone inlay at the southern end of the park), swinging by (6) **Jefferson's Residence** (page 19) to see the commemorative plaque there on the way.

If you have some extra time, you can head to **Bayard's Mansion** (page 27) (either on your way downtown or on your way back uptown), to see the plaque commemorating where Hamilton was taken after the duel with Burr and where he died. The mansion is just over a quarter-mile walk from the subway station.

Daddy said not to go downtown...

Uptown

Start at (1) *the Grange* (page 23), and expect to spend at least two hours there if you go on a tour (either ranger-led or self-guided). Try to take a walk around the grounds if you have time – it can get crowded but is still quite peaceful. You can then swing by (2) St. Luke's Episcopal Church to see a statue of Alexander Hamilton (the Grange was acquired by the church in the late 1800s and temporarily moved to the grounds) and then head over to (3) *Morris-Jumel Mansion* (page 35), which is either a 1.1 mile walk or a 10-15 minute bus ride (walk over to St. Nicholas Avenue and take the M3 uptown – you can use your Metrocard). If you are interested in a tour, visit morrisjumel.org for a schedule – there are only about a half-dozen docent-led tours per month.

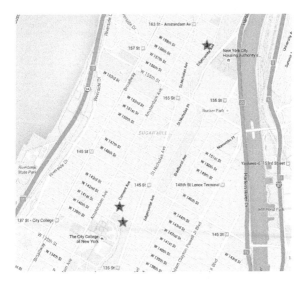

If you have time, head over to the 157th Street subway station to take the 1 train downtown to 116th Street, where you can visit the campus of Columbia University – *King's College* (page 15) is now Columbia College. There you can see a statue of Alexander Hamilton in front of Hamilton Hall.

It's quiet uptown...

Central Park Area

Start at (1) the ***New-York Historical Society*** (page 42), where you can see statues depicting the Hamilton-Burr duel, as well as several other Hamilton artifacts (the museum also houses artifacts and documents from the collection of the Gilder Lehrman Institute of American History, including a copy of the Reynolds Pamphlet – note that these documents are not on permanent display). The museum also held a Summer of Hamilton exhibit in the summer of 2016, with special Hamilton-related exhibits and events (hopefully this will become an annual event). If the weather is nice, take a walk across Central Park (three-quarters of a mile) to see (2) the statue of Alexander Hamilton (the statue was donated to the park in 1880 by Hamilton's son, John). From there you can head another mile uptown to (3) the ***Museum of the City of New York*** (page 44), where you can see portraits of Revolution-era historical figures, including Hamilton and George Washington. If it's a nice day and you have time, head over to (4) the Conservatory Garden (enter between 104th/105th Streets; open 8AM to dusk) - no connection with Hamilton, but a beautiful garden to take a walk through (while listening to *Hamilton*?).

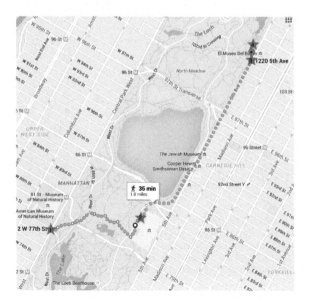

Hamilton's Final Hours

Start in *Weehawken, NJ* (page 47), where Aaron Burr mortally wounded Alexander Hamilton during their duel on July 11, 1804. From there head to *Bayard's Mansion* (page 27), where Hamilton was taken following the duel and where he died the following day (with Eliza and Angelica at his side).

His funeral procession and burial were two days later, on July 14th. To follow the path of the procession, start from (1) the home of John and Angelica Church (Schuyler) and walk over to (2) *the Common* (page 11). The procession then wound along Beekman Street and down Pearl Street, taking you near (3) *Stone Street* (page 31), where Hamilton once had an office, and past (4) *Fraunces Tavern* (page 9) – either location would be a good place to stop for a drink or a meal if you need a break. Finally, head up Whitehall Street, going past the former site of (5) Fort George in *the Battery* (page 13) and then up Broadway past (6) *26 Broadway* (page 29), where Hamilton once lived, to (7) *Trinity Church* (page 25), where Hamilton was eulogized and laid to rest (and where you can pay your respects to Hamilton, among others).

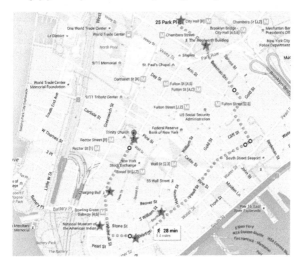

Unless you rush through it, this itinerary will take most of a day, so you may want to skip Weehawken if you only have half a day.

I hear wailing in the streets...

If You're More of a Burr Fan

This itinerary will take you all over the city and will require a full day unless you skip some portions (I've grouped together the locations that are near each other (Uptown, Downtown, SoHo and New Jersey) – skip an entire group if you're pressed for time). Since this itinerary covers so much area, I decided not to include a map – go to the individual pages for location information. Note that Federal Hall is closed Saturdays (except during the Summer) and Sundays and that Morris-Jumel Mansion is closed Mondays.

Start in New Jersey, at *Weehawken* (page 47), the site of Aaron Burr's famous duel with Alexander Hamilton (which branded Burr as *the villain in your history…*).

Next head Downtown, where Burr and Hamilton saw action in the American Revolution. Start at *Federal Hall* (page 21), where Burr and Hamilton defended Levi Weeks, then head over to *Fraunces Tavern* (page 9). Don't forget to make a reservation (see page 9) if you want to have lunch there. Take the half-mile walk up to *the Common* (page 11) to burn off some of your lunch.

Now go Uptown to *Morris-Jumel Mansion* (page 35). The easiest way to get there is to take the C train from Chambers Street uptown to 163rd Street, but if you're familiar with the subway it's faster to take the A train and then switch to the C (or the 2/3 uptown from Park Place and switch to the 1 train). Going here next may seem a bit out of order, but you need to get there and have time to look around before the mansion closes at 4PM (or 5PM on the weekends).

Finally, head down to SoHo for a couple of quick site visits. You can either take the 1 train from 157th Street downtown to Houston Street or the C train from 163rd Street downtown to Spring Street. Walk through the Charlton-King-Vandam Historic District, where the *Richmond Hill* (page 17) estate was once located (though there's nothing specific to see other than the Federal-style row houses that are now there). Now walk west to finish your day at the *COS Clothing Store* (page 43). In the basement of the store is the haunted well where the murder victim in the Levi Weeks trial was found. Not only was Burr part of the defense team for the trial, but the well was located on land owned by the Manhattan Company, which was founded by Burr as a bank to compete with Hamilton's Bank of New York.

I'm willing to wait for it…

If you have one or more full days, you can start to think about seeing almost everything in Manhattan or even heading out of the city. Each bullet point below should take about a day, so combine them if you have more time and want to see more.

- **Combinations of Half-Day Itineraries**

  You can combine any two of the half-day itineraries (pages 63-65). Note that the Central Park itinerary leaves you on the Upper East Side, so if you're going to combine this with the Uptown itinerary, start with Uptown.

- **Themed Itineraries**

  You also have time for either of the themed itineraries (pages 66 and 67), including a break to eat at *Fraunces Tavern* (page 9).

- **Farther Afield in New Jersey**

  Consider visiting *Morristown* (page 49), *Elizabethtown* (page 53), *Paterson* (page 55), or the *Battle of Monmouth* (page 51).

  Morristown – The train to Morristown takes about 80 minutes (each way, to and from Penn Station – see page 49 for details).

  Elizabethtown – The train to Elizabeth takes about 30 minutes (each way, to and from Penn Station – see page 53 for details).

  Paterson – The bus to Paterson takes about 45 minutes (each way, to and from Port Authority – see page 55 for details).

  Battle of Monmouth – If you have a car, just plug "Monmouth Battlefield State Park" into your GPS and go; it's about a 70-80 minute drive (each way, from Times Square). If you don't have a car, it will take you about 2-1/2 hours to get there by bus (from Port Authority) and walking (this includes a 1.3 mile walk from the bus stop in New Jersey (the Freehold Raceway Mall stop), so assume more time if you're a slow walker).

- **Pennsylvania**

  As you can see on page 59, many events depicted in *Hamilton: An American Musical* occurred in or around Philadelphia. George Washington's Continental Army battled in and around Philadelphia (and spent harsh winters in nearby Valley Forge). Alexander Hamilton spent much of his tenure as Treasury Secretary at the temporary government located in Philadelphia (and this was where he "had a torrid affair" with Maria Reynolds). This book does not provide any location information about these sites, so you're on your own (but please share any information on these sites at Info@wwtrwih.com).

ACKNOWLEDGEMENTS

First and foremost, the inspiration for this book was clearly *Hamilton: An American Musical*. While credit for the show goes mainly to Lin-Manuel Miranda, I think that the show is also made by the incredibly talented men and women that perform the show every night (consider that as of the time I wrote this book, I've seen the show twice and still have not seen Miranda perform, and it's still the best show I've ever seen). Standouts for me are Leslie Odom, Jr., Daveed Diggs, Christopher Jackson, Jonathan Groff, Phillipa Soo and Renee Elise Goldsberry. They have together created something wonderful – it's amazing to me that such a huge community has developed around the show, and that it has been able to bridge across so many different groups of people.

Second would be Ron Chernow, whose biography *Alexander Hamilton* opened my eyes about the connections between the show and the locations where the events took place. I initially tried to give attribution in the book wherever Chernow's book was the source of my info, but it didn't layout well. But please note that much of the info in this book is based upon Chernow's biography.

Third is the Alexander Hamilton Awareness Society (AHA), with a special thanks to their president, Rand Scholet. Scholet provided a final set of eyes to confirm the historical accuracy of the book, and he was responsible for the addition of a few of the locations. AHA's support for the book, and their welcoming of me into the Hamilton community, have been especially gratifying. I would also like to thank Nicole Scholet de Villavicencio, who helped with images, promotion and my web presence, and Leonard A. Zax, who was instrumental in getting Paterson, N.J. in this book.

Most important are my family – my kids London and Andrew and especially my wife, Rebecca. Without their support and encouragement I may have never started this book, and I definitely would never have finished it. I also want to thank my mother-in-law, Jean Couban, whose enthusiasm helped keep me going when I was down about my failed Kickstarter campaign for this book.

Finally I want to thank everyone who supported my book, from the few who supported the Kickstarter campaign (Erynn Albert, John Bode, Thad Bzomowski, Ryan Carey, David Cohn, Jean Couban, Lucas Deshouillers, Cindy Elder, Julien Gimbrere, Adam Greene, Trey Key, Ger Laffan, Mike Loos, Rob O'Connell, Marissa Tai and Jerry Walrath) to Topher Horn and David Montoya, who gave me needed advice about putting a book together. And I want to throw shout outs to Gary Vaynerchuk (I don't know him but I took his message of hustling to heart in putting in the time and work to get this done), and Jimmy Napoli, Carol Ward, Richard Brookhiser and Doug Hamilton, who have helped me get the book out there.

Thanks for everything – I couldn't have done this without you!

IMAGE CREDITS

All photographs included in this book were taken by me (using my iPhone 6-plus) except for the following photographs, drawings or paintings:

Page 9, Fraunces Tavern – By Jim Henderson (Own work) [Public domain], via Wikimedia Commons (from Wikipedia page); cropped by B.L. Barreras

Page 17, Richmond Hill – By Charles Haynes Haswell; cropped by Beyond My Ken (talk) 20:39, 19 June 2011 (UTC) - NYPL Digital Gallery [Public domain]

Page 21, Federal Hall – Archibald Robertson's "View up Wall Street" w/City Hall - [Public domain], via Wikimedia Commons

Page 23, The Grange – By OH.F. Langmann [Public domain], via Wikimedia Commons

Page 35, Morris-Jumel Mansion – By Beyond My Ken (Own work) [GFDL (http://www.gnu.org/copyleft/fdl.html) or CC BY-SA 4.0-3.0-2.5-2.0-1.0 (http://creativecommons.org/licenses/by-sa/4.0-3.0-2.5-2.0-1.0)], via Wikimedia Commons

Page 47, Aaron-Burr Duel – By Illustrator not identified. From a painting by J. Mund. [Public domain], via Wikimedia Commons

Page 49, Ford Mansion – photograph by National Park Service employee created as part of the employee's duties [Public domain]

Page 51, Battle of Monmouth – Emanuel Leutze painted Washington Rallying the Troops at Monmouth [Public domain], via Wikimedia Commons

Page 53, The Snyder Academy of Elizabethtown – By Nicole Scholet de Villavicencio (Own work), the Alexander Hamilton Awareness Society, with permission; cropped by B.L. Barreras

Page 55, Paterson Great Falls – photographer unknown, from the collection of Leonard A. Zax, with permission

Page 59, First Bank of the United States – By Nicole Scholet de Villavicencio (Own work), the Alexander Hamilton Awareness Society, with permission; cropped by B.L. Barreras

SOURCE CREDITS

As mentioned under "Acknowledgements", I initially tried to include source attributions throughout the book, but it didn't really fit well with the layout of the book (and this is more of a tour guidebook than a history book, though I did spend a lot of time getting the history part correct). So rather than fact-by-fact attribution, I would like to instead recognize the sources that I used for this book.

First and foremost is Ron Chernow's *Alexander Hamilton* biography, which provided a lot of date information necessary to tie the events depicted in *Hamilton: An American Musical* to the locations where they occurred.

The timing of publication of *Hamilton: The Revolution*, by Lin-Manuel Miranda and Jeremy McCarter was fortuitous, as it helped me confirm some of the setting info for the show. And I very much enjoyed *Duel with the Devil: The True Story of How Alexander Hamilton and Aaron Burr Teamed Up to Take on America's First Sensational Murder Mystery*, by Paul Collins – while this did not provide much information for this book, it was key in sparking my intrigue about where events from Hamilton's life happened (since the trial occurred at Federal Hall, which had previously been the seat of the federal government).

Beyond these books, my research was done online and onsite. Where I provided information about visiting a location, I tried to get this information from the actual location (e.g., pamphlets or displays) for the New York City locations or directly from the website for the location (and I similarly tried to take historical information directly from that location or website, though this was often not provided). I also tried where possible to verify information that I obtained online against Chernow's book. The images other than my own photographs and those provided by the Alexander Hamilton Awareness Society were all obtained through Wikipedia, primarily because it was the most direct source of public domain images (due to the site's own guidelines for posting images on the site).

Further descriptions and photographs for each site can be found at www.AllPlacesHamilton.com. For recent and future events at Alexander Hamilton locations, in addition to the sites included in this book visit www.theAHAsociety.org. Both websites are provided by the Alexander Hamilton Awareness Society.

INDEX

INDEX BY SONG TITLE

ACT II

ORDERING ADDITIONAL GUIDES AND EBOOK

Additional guides can be ordered online (Amazon or B&N) or purchased at retail locations (www.wwtrwih.com has a list of locations). Email me at Info@wwtrwih.com for bulk orders or to carry the book in your store. The book can also be customized (with your company color and/or logo on the cover) for corporate gifts - email me at Info@wwtrwih.com for further information.

This book is also available as an eBook (Amazon, iTunes, B&N, Smashwords) - search by title, visit www.wwtrwih.com for links, or use the QR codes below. As the images below show, the eBook has hyper-links to navigate you through the book (and to external websites), as well as zoomable fonts, maps and pictures.

Amazon QR Code:

iTunes QR Code:

THANKS SO MUCH FOR READING MY BOOK!

CPSIA information can be obtained
at www.ICGtesting.com
Printed in the USA
LVOW06s1415130916
504413LV00019B/181/P